The Quest
for Meaning

Also by Jim Rosemergy

Books

A Closer Walk With God
A Daily Guide to Spiritual Living
A Recent Revelation
Even Mystics Have Bills to Pay
Living the Mystical Life Today
The Watcher
The Sacred Human
The Transcendent Life

Cassette Albums

What Unity Teaches
*Raising Children or Raising Consciousness,
   Which?*
The Science of Prayer
From Metaphysics to Mysticism
*How to Win the Human Race: Lessons in
   Unconditional Love*
*The Cornerstone of a New World: Personal and
   Planetary Change*
Awakening Spiritual Consciousness
*Famous Bible Stories From the Old Testament:
   A Mystical View*
Living the Mystical Life Today

The Quest for Meaning

Living a Life of Purpose

Jim Rosemergy

UNITY® Books

Unity Village, Missouri

First Edition 1999

Published by the Unity Movement Advisory Council, a joint committee of the Association of Unity Churches and Unity School of Christianity.

To receive a catalog of all Unity publications (books, cassettes, and magazines) or to place an order, call the Customer Service Department: 1-800-669-0282 or (816) 969-2069.

Bible quotations are from the Revised Standard Version unless otherwise noted.

Cover design by Melody Burns

Library of Congress Cataloging-in-Publication Data:
Rosemergy, Jim.
    The quest for meaning : living a life of purpose / Jim Rosemergy.
        p.   cm.
    ISBN 0-87159-222-3
    1. Spiritual life—Unity School of Christianity. 2. Unity School of Christianity—Doctrines.   I. Title.
BX9890.U505R65   1998
248.4'8997—dc21   98-18423
                                                                      CIP

Unity Books feels a sacred trust to be a healing presence in the world. By printing with biodegradable soybean ink on recycled paper, we believe we are doing our part to be wise stewards of our Earth's resources.

Publisher's Note

The books in this series continue the work started by *The Quest* and *Adventures on the Quest* by Mary-Alice and Richard Jafolla. *The Quest* has succeeded in fulfilling its original objectives by effectively presenting an overview of Unity philosophical perspectives and basic beliefs. It also has provided Unity churches and centers a vehicle for individual spiritual growth as well as supported community-building by encouraging intergenerational sharing and personal bonding. *The Quest* offered a planned, yearlong exercise in commitment, instruction, and focused learning.

While *The Quest* remains viable in its original form, this new series of books intends a more advanced application of its concept. This series offers a more topic-specific focus and a small-book format adaptable to a shorter course of instruction. The series assumes a basic familiarity with *The Quest* teachings.

All the books in this series are endorsed by the Unity Movement Advisory Council, a joint committee of the Association of Unity Churches and Unity School of Christianity.

Table of Contents

Preface

A decade ago I could not have written the book you are about to read, because in past years my quest for meaning meandered like an ancient river—first moving in one direction and then another. At times, athletic endeavors seemed to make life meaningful. Later, academic pursuits seemed important, and of course, romance often made my heart sing. As my life unfolded, career took front and center. Now, as I look back, it is easy to see that I had not looked inside myself to discover my purpose or to find meaning. I must have been thoroughly convinced that the world held all the treasures I would ever need. The challenge was how to get them.

I do not condemn myself for the journey that I have taken. In many ways, it has opened my eyes, for now I see that my primary fault was in taking the path trod by the masses. I looked for meaning and purpose in what I did, what I acquired, and what others said about me. My way of achieving these things was to "take thought" for my life. After all, thoughts held in mind will produce after their kind. Through the use of spiritual principles as I understood them, I tried to "make it happen," and I succeeded. However, a funny thing happened on

the way to success, meaning, and purpose. There
was no fulfillment. Something was missing, and I
did not know what it was.

I was puzzled. My life was full, or so I thought,
but then I discovered that it was not full of God. It
was full of earthly treasures that do not endure. I
was alive, but not living a life of purpose.

About ten years ago, the quest for the missing
piece, God, began in earnest and with it the quest
for meaning. Now I believe there is no meaning,
fulfillment, or purpose without a conscious awareness of God. All things begin with Spirit. Now I
have finally taken one of Jesus' statements to heart:
"Therefore take no thought, saying, What shall we
eat? or, What shall we drink? or, Wherewithal shall
we be clothed? . . . But seek ye first the kingdom of
God, and his righteousness; and all these things
shall be added unto you" (Mt. 6:31, 33 KJV).

The meandering has ceased. All is not clear, but
a clear direction has been set. You will see it in this
book. The quest for meaning is first a quest for
God. You are asked to put Jesus' statement to the
test and not take thought for your life, but instead
to seek to know and experience the Presence. Admittedly, this is a path that is not as well-known or
well-worn as the "take thought" approach to living
and meaning, but I can assure you it is worthy of
your commitment.

Dear friend, you have been searching for meaning and purpose all your life. We all do. It is as natural for us to ask why we are here as it is for a flower to turn to the light of the morning sun. So let us cease our meandering and turn to the light, and we will find that our quest for meaning is actually our quest for God. When we find God, we find ourselves—our purpose—and finally our lives have meaning.

Introduction

To Dance With
the Question *Why?*

It started long ago, when our species first achieved consciousness. A distant kinsman awakened—*I am*. This uneducated forerunner of the human species must have grasped what René Descartes came to realize: *"Cogito, ergo sum;* I think, therefore I am."

With self-consciousness came a question. *I am, but what am I?* Each culture has answered this question through its myths, oral traditions, and eventually through its sacred literature. Simply stated, we named ourselves. We are human beings, we are spiritual beings, we are children of the sun, people of the High Place, and so on. Individuality, of course, required a personal name: I am Jim or I am Soars Like an Eagle or I am Friend of the Wind or I am Mary. We named ourselves, knowing that words do not adequately describe what we are. Then another question came, far-reaching and powerful in its possibilities, a question that each of us asks, usually in the night—*Why am I?*

Hasn't nearly every human being stood alone and looked at the clear night sky? In that moment, gazing into the cosmos, we can feel small. Sometimes, however, a cosmic experience may cause us to feel a part of everything. At other times, when storm clouds encircle us and we are greatly challenged by life's circumstances, we can feel detached from the whole and without value. Either at peace looking into the night sky or anxious and afraid of tomorrow, we often dance with the question *Why?* Why are we here? We are turned and spun round by such questions as these: *Does life have meaning? Is there a purpose for being? Can I make a difference?* Without answers, life is aimless and each day can be drudgery.

Astronomers spend their lives gazing into the clear night sky. They say they are looking for clues to the origin of the earth and the universe, but isn't it the origin and why of our species that begs to be answered? These scientists are the offspring of a race of beings who have stood alone and searched the heavens. The ancient ones looked up, but they yearned for meaning on earth. I think it is interesting to speculate that the first of our species asked the same questions we ask today: *What am I? Why am I? Does life have meaning and purpose?*

If we are solely human beings, then a central purpose would be to continue. We are to live as long as we can and perpetuate the race. Extinction would be the enemy. However, we are spiritual beings. There is no end to us. We are eternal, and this is vital, for it often takes what seems like an eternity for us to discover our purpose and value.

My hope is that what is shared through this book will help us discover our reason for being. To even consider such a breakthrough fills me with anticipation and hope. And the hope is not just for you and me; it is for our species. Surely, our individual lives have purpose, but when we are all joined in a unity of purpose, something wonderful is going to happen.

We live in an intelligent universe. Our Creator must have a grand purpose for our being. I believe that when we discover it, our values will shift and our evolution will take a new direction, a direction that Spirit has ordained. A doorway to the kingdom of God will form, through which the Presence will emerge. Creativity will rule the day, and compassion will rule the night.

So, even though we may stumble, let us dance with the question *Why?* Let us turn and spin in harmony with the music of the spheres. And in the joy of the dance, I believe we will discover that our lives have purpose and that we can make a difference.

Chapter One

Our Unity of Purpose

A Child Is Born

A child is born. The mother tenderly holds the newborn in her arms, and the father peers at their daughter through eyes moistened with tears. Although filled with the wonder and mystery of birth, each parent silently ponders the mystery of life. What will our child be? What will she do? Will she be a teacher, a lawyer, a minister, an engineer, and so forth? Will she work with her hands or will her mind be her tool? Will she contribute to the lives of others? Will the world be a better place because she lived?

Life, being, truly is a miracle—not a random act, but the conception of a divine Mind and the outworking of a divine plan. Now, consider the Creator of all life, cradling the family in Its arms and pondering the birth of this child: *The parents, man and woman, conceived this child, but first she was an idea in My mind and love in My heart. This one who is called a newborn is eternal and part of the divine plan. She has earthly parents and will dwell upon the*

earth in a body for a while, but she is made in My
image and likeness. The parents will name her, but I
call her beloved and her nature spiritual. For a while,
she will be human, but always she will be a spiritual
being, not only with the ability to contribute to the
lives of others, but also with the capacity to allow Me
to express Myself in and through and as her. She is!
She has life and being. I have breathed into her. I
have spoken her name, and My word has become
flesh. May she discover why she lives!

The Gift of God

The gift of God is nearly beyond belief, for Spirit
gives Itself to us. "You are Mine, I am yours, and we
are one," says our Creator. From this giving and
oneness come life and being. Spirit breathes into
us, and we become living beings. God speaks, and
the Word becomes flesh.

So first, there is the gift of God which becomes
life and being, and then another gift is given—purpose, the gift which makes life meaningful. And
out of our purpose comes a mission that will uncover our talents and latent abilities. In fact, our
mission will demand that we utilize our special
gifts. We will have work to do, but it will be our joy.
When we do it, we will feel God's pleasure.

When we have purpose, we are enlivened and
live life with boundless energy. Each day is an ad-

venture and an opportunity to make our unique contribution to the divine plan. Purpose calls forth creativity. It opens a gateway to infinite resources that lie within—wisdom, peace, power, love, and strength.

We will give our lives to our purpose and our mission. It is not so much that we will die for them, although we may, as it is that we will live for them. When we have purpose and mission, we feel part of the whole. We know ourselves to be a part of something greater than ourselves. Only an awareness of the Presence can connect us with the whole in such a powerful way. It is God that is the something greater, and therefore, we must turn to the Presence if we are to find our purpose and our mission.

A Part of Something Greater

Sir Christopher Wren was a British architect who designed and built great cathedrals. One day he was walking through a construction site and talking to the workers. They did not know who he was. Wren asked a man what he was making. The mason answered, "I am making a shilling a day." To a second worker, Wren posed the same question. He answered, "I am building a wall." When Wren asked a third person what he was doing, the man proudly stood up and said to the stranger who was wandering the construction site, "I am helping Sir Christopher Wren build the greatest cathedral in the world."

The third man had vision. His mission was not making money, nor was it the task at hand. He had an expanded view of himself and the world. I suspect he was a happy man, for the happiest, most contented, and fulfilled individuals are those who live in a large world. They refuse to be limited to the task at hand or to what they receive for their efforts. They know their labor is united to something greater. They feel God's pleasure and joy as they work.

Jesus, A Child of Purpose

At age 12, Jesus knew his purpose. Joseph and Mary had traveled with Jesus to Jerusalem to celebrate the Passover. The festivities were complete, and the family was returning to Nazareth. Jesus' parents assumed he was in the crowd that was homeward bound. After a time, they realized their son was not with them. Mary and Joseph returned to the Holy City, and after searching for three days, they found Jesus in the temple discussing spiritual matters with the elders. When Jesus was admonished by his parents for his behavior, he answered, "Did you not know that I must be about My Father's business?" (Lk. 2:49 NKJV)

Jesus lived a life of purpose, and consequently he lived one of the most extraordinary lives that has ever been lived. He became aware of the divine intent and made it his own. His initial effort was to discover the Presence within him. Having found his Father closer to him than his own hands and feet and his own breathing, Jesus next became aware of the divine plan and became a partner in it.

Our Spiritual Purpose

A journey to a life of meaning causes us to consider our spiritual purpose, to discover our mission, to uncover our latent abilities, and finally to find our life's work. If we are to live a life of meaning and contribute constructively to the world, we must first discover our spiritual purpose.

Those things that are spiritual must be the same for everyone, for Spirit has no favorites. All are held in equal esteem. What is offered is offered to everyone. The Truth is that everyone has the same spiritual purpose. There are different ways of expressing it, but our spiritual purpose is to know God and to experience the Presence.

Many years ago, I went to a log cabin in the woods to determine if I could write constantly for a period of three days. I had felt guided to do this for a long time. I entered the cabin, got a fire going in the fireplace, and set up my 64K Kaypro com-

puter on a card table near a picture window looking out over a mountain lake.

I began to write. After having written only two
paragraphs, the cursor on the computer locked up.
I ran my hand over the keys. Nothing happened. I
removed the disc that contained the word process-
ing program and inserted it again. (I told you it
was many years ago.) The cursor continued to
blink at me.

I liked what I had written, so I copied it longhand
and shut off the computer, then brought it on-line
again. Nothing changed. At this point, I began to realize why a cursor is called a cursor. Having lost my
sense of an indwelling God, I looked up and said,
"God, for years I have felt Your guidance to come
and write. Finally, I am here, and the computer
locks up."

It was one of those times when I heard a distinct
voice reply, "Your purpose is not to write; it is to
know Me." Shocked, I returned to my computer,
and the cursor moved.

I wrote for three days. Nothing ever came of the
words written, but I never forgot Spirit's simple
message: Know Me. This event changed my life and
gave me purpose. It also demanded that I change
the focus of my life.

I have a friend who had a similar experience.
After more than forty years, she found her birth

mother. After the meeting of mother and daughter, my friend was changed forever, "in the twinkling of an eye" (1 Cor. 15:52). She had a deeper sense of who she was. She remarked that she felt grounded for the first time in her life.

Humanly, something wonderful often happens when an orphaned child discovers his father or mother. Imagine what happens when we finally find our Creator. Just like my friend, we know ourselves better and are better able to live. And since our Creator is infinite, our spiritual purpose is always with us. It is like a friendship between people. There is no completion. The friendship grows and deepens. It expands to encompass the love that wells up in the hearts of the friends.

This is the way I feel about my relationship with the Presence. It is an emerging friendship that I know will one day meld into oneness. To say that one's spiritual purpose is to know God is somewhat accurate, but words never tell the whole story. Knowing God is not a matter of the mind, for Spirit cannot be known the way we know our hometown. It is more a matter of love, of friendship. This purpose is of the heart.

Isn't it true that friendship helps us know ourselves? Surely, we know our friend better each day, and we love him or her more each day, but in the loving, we find ourselves. Our spiritual purpose expands us and reveals a portion of the mystery of being. We know God; we love God, and we come to love ourselves and others, in spite of faults. Can we say that we are done with this, that we know all we can know of the Presence and ourselves? Of course not. Our purpose is a constant companion that gives meaning to our lives.

Spirit Calls Us to Purpose

Spirit calls us to purpose: "Be still, and know" (Ps. 46:10). "You shall love the Lord your God with all your heart, and with all your soul, and with all your mind, and with all your strength" (Mk. 12:30). However, we often ignore the Creator's call and propose that God perform for us. We want the Almighty to do Its mighty thing: "Heal me, God" or "Get me a job" or "What do I do in this situation? Tell me" or "Can you find me someone who will love me? I am praying for the right and perfect person!"

The experience of our spiritual purpose does not come when we give attention to the world and its added things. If we were solely human beings, then worldly concerns and their fruits would be enough, but we are *not* just human beings. We are spiritual beings, created so the Creator can express Itself in, through, and *as* us.

Spirit's call is lofty and beyond human imagining, but as we respond to Spirit's yearning for us, earthly needs that seem so all-consuming are met without making them the object of our existence. "But seek first his kingdom and his righteousness, and all these things shall be yours as well" (Mt. 6:33). This is a promise as well as a challenge—to live a new way of life, one worthy of a being of the third millennium.

I can say to you that your spiritual purpose is to know God and love God and also to know yourself, but this alone will have no effect on your life. You must *experience* your spiritual purpose. Because your *why* is not of the earth, you must "sit with the elders." This does not mean you must find wise ones who will impart their wisdom to you. "Sitting with the elders" means quiet reflection that allows the voice still and small to speak to you. It means listening to inner voices. Some will be human in nature. You won't like what they say, but there is a loving, gentle "voice" that you are destined to experience. For now, gently lay aside your worldly concerns. When you return to them, they will look different, but *they* are not the issue now. Experiencing your spiritual purpose is the matter at hand.

Sitting With the Elders

When we seek the kingdom of God, we give ourselves to the Presence; we are sitting with the elders, as Jesus did long ago. The spiritual purpose is the same for every human being—we want to

know our roots, our Creator, our God. This is our
first step—to ask, to seek, to knock. At this time, it
is not necessary to know, to find, or to enter into a
conscious awareness of the Presence. The journey
to purpose begins with right desire. It is enough, for
our willingness to experience the Presence or become a friend of God marshals spiritual forces that
grant many gifts.

No matter what is happening in our daily lives,
we can give ourselves to knowing the Presence.
When we are unemployed, we have the work of
awakening to our spiritual nature. When we are ill,
we are being called to know God as life. No matter
the challenge, our purpose is to know God; however, when we catch our breath and are momen-
tarily free of challenges and problems, we still have
the joyous responsibility of knowing the Presence
and sharing in the divine friendship.

As we seek the kingdom, we open ourselves to
the divine intent to which we can give our lives.
Through the years, it has been revealed to people in
different ways, and it is evident that there is a special quality about a person who knows his purpose
and mission.

The Divine Pattern

On September 10, 1946, a young nun was on a
train traveling to her annual retreat. Her purpose

was to know God and love God. Her ongoing re-
treats were evidence that she knew the spiritual
purpose which is the same for all of us. While on
the train, Agnes Gonxha Bojaxhiu, who was to become Mother Teresa of Calcutta, heard her "call
within a call"—to take care of the sick, dying,
naked, homeless, and hungry. She knew she was
being asked to be God's love in action to the poorest of the poor. This was the beginning of the Mis-
sionaries of Charity.

She did not hesitate. She asked to establish a
new order to work in the deprived areas of India.
At 38 years of age, she left the convent where she
was a teacher to begin the new order. She knew
her purpose: to know God. Now she had a God-
mission: to be God's love in action.

One who knew her as a novice in the order of the
Sisters of Our Lady of Loreto said she couldn't even
light the candles properly, but after her call, her latent talents and abilities began to show themselves.
This is true of those who seek the kingdom. They
give themselves to the spiritual purpose and a God-
mission arises. The mission is the "call within a
call." Then latent talents and abilities emerge.

It was this way with Albert Schweitzer. At the
age of twenty-one, Schweitzer decided to spend the
next nine years developing his mind and talents. He
determined that during the remaining years of his

life, he would serve humanity. He also continued formal education, however, and in 1913 obtained a doctorate in medicine from the University of Strasbourg. Schweitzer then traveled to Lambaréné in French Equatorial Africa (now Gabon). Until he died on September 4, 1965, Dr. Schweitzer served humankind and through example taught reverence for life.

People of purpose have heard the call to know God. As they experience this calling, they receive a "call within a call" that focuses their life's purpose upon their God-mission. The mission places great demands upon the person—demands that cannot be met unless talents and abilities emerge. The divine intent is expressed through their work, and humankind is blessed beyond measure.

All people have the same spiritual purpose: to know God, to love God, and to know themselves. This is our unity of purpose, and when we make it our reason for being, we hear the call within the call.

Mile Markers

- All human beings share a common spiritual purpose.
- The journey to purpose begins with right desire.
- Our spiritual purpose can be expressed in numerous ways, but essentially it is to experience the Presence.
- Spirit desires to express Itself in us, through us, and *as* us.
- Purpose opens a gateway to infinite resources that lie within—wisdom, peace, power, love, and strength.
- Through purpose, our desire for God and God's desire for us are wed in perfect unity.
- Spiritual purpose is the underlying force of our lives.
- People of purpose receive a God-mission that calls forth hidden and latent abilities and talents.

Adventure One

Our Unity of Purpose

The real search of all people is for God. They may think they are looking for other things, but they must eventually admit that it is God they seek.

—Charles Fillmore

One of our greatest adventures is the search for meaning. Throughout the ages, myths and legends have been told and retold about pilgrimages, holy commissions, and the search for such treasures as the Holy Grail. To complete the quest or to find the treasure is to find what is most precious in our lives. I believe the chalice that Jesus drank from was purpose. The quest is to live a life of meaning.

This cup is offered to you. You have embarked upon the eternal quest that calls every creation of God. When you hold the chalice in your hands, and you will, look into its depth and you will find your reason for being. Press the cup to your lips and drink deeply—of life, of purpose, and of meaning.

Soul-Talk

My life has purpose. Write this declaration three times, pausing between each line to allow the statement to saturate your consciousness. Then say it aloud or silently as many times as you can each day during this Adventure.

1. _____

2. _____

3. _____

Soul-Thoughts

After you have completed writing your Soul-Talk, take time to sit quietly and observe your thoughts and feelings. Write them down.

1. *What have you believed to be your reason for being?*

2. Often a person who discovers that he or she was orphaned as an infant feels a loss of identity. As spiritual beings not knowing our Creator, we have feelings of a similar nature. Perhaps you have felt these feelings when you have been spiritually lost or alone. *What feelings, thoughts, or beliefs did you experience?*

3. *If you had been one of the workers whom Sir Christopher Wren spoke to as he toured the cathedral building site, which of the three workers would you have been and why?*

4. *If your spiritual purpose is to know God, what will you do to open yourself to this experience?*

5. *As you experience life during the next seven days, remember that your purpose is to know God.* Every situation can be a reminder of our spiritual quest.

Off the Main Trail

During the next week, write in 25 words or less a brief description of the lives of the three people who responded to Sir Christopher Wren's question, "What are you making?" In other words, what is life like for a person who works for money, who tries to derive meaning from what he does, or whose work is a contribution to a greater vision?

Stepping-Stone

During the time you read and study *The Quest for Meaning*, research an auto-biography of a person who has made a powerful contribution to the human family. Look for the time when the individual discovered his or her mission. Chapter Two, "A Call Within a Call," will help you in your research.

My life has purpose.

Chapter Two

A Call Within a Call

Stargates

God yearns for us, and eventually we greet this yearning with a desire to know God and discover what it means to be made in the image of the Creator. The Truth is that we are made for conscious union with the Divine and without it we feel incomplete. Earthly treasures and fruits may seem to fulfill us for a time, but the void of not knowing the Presence and ourselves remains. We are spiritual orphans, who must eventually search for the One who gave us life.

And there is more. Not only are we engineered to experience oneness with the Presence, but we are created so Spirit can express Itself in and through and as us. We are doors, stargates, through which the divine light may shine and illumine a shadowy world.

Our purpose is cosmic. We are created so God will have hands through which to act and voices through which to speak. The love of Spirit must not remain an unrealized potential. The divine plan demands that divine love assume its rightful place as the center of our lives. We are to love one another and care for those in need.

Those who are partners in this plan, those who are willing to allow Spirit to express Itself, claim nothing that emerges from within them, for they know they of themselves can do nothing. What they witness being birthed from within their souls is conceived in the womb of God rather than in their own minds.

These are the possibilities and the implications of our conception and birth. The question is, How will we respond to God's yearning for expression? Will we ignore it and look to the world to fill the void we feel inside? Most of us attempt to find meaning in what we acquire, what we do, and what others say about us. This is normal. It is part of the rite of passage involved in the journey to meaning and purpose. But the day comes when we realize that these things have not caused the void and our feeling of incompleteness to go away. Still, something is missing!

The Search for Meaning

As I began to write this book, a friend came to me and told me of his search for purpose, meaning, and mission. He said he was leaving his work for a time to try to find himself and something that he knew was missing from his life. How many people feel this same void, but plow ahead in hopes of a future harvest? They live lives of despair and "quiet desperation" (Thoreau). They breathe, they exist, but the breath of God never fills them. They do not know their purpose and what God created them to be.

My friend refused to live a meaningless life. He knew the void and felt incomplete. In essence, he was feeling God's yearning for him, and I was privileged to see him respond. He announced he was taking a sabbatical from his work in order to truly feel his purpose and find his mission. He sought a new vision for his life.

I thoroughly supported my friend's search for meaning. His initiative was an inspiration to me and an act of courage. From his standpoint, he had no choice. Only a divine revelation would free him.

Vision Quest

Native Americans understood the need and power of revelation. Many tribes had their youth embark upon a vision quest. Some cultures believed that unless one had a spiritual experience during the quest, life would be without meaning. Each tribe or nation approached the quest for meaning in a unique way, but most practices endorsed a need to say no to the world. There were

often purification rites and fasting. The physical
forces of the body were weakened to create a
greater sensitivity to spiritual energies. The one
who sought the revelation was alone, and some de-
gree of danger was allowed.

The vision quest acknowledged the unseen dimension of life. I believe all of us feel the tug of
mystery and spiritual forces. We sense that we are
more than we appear to be and that behind all form
is a greater reality. Like orphans, we wonder about
the One who gave us birth.

The one seeking the vision, or as we would say,
"an experience of the Presence," knew this was potentially the beginning of a relationship that would
culminate with the person feeling a part of the
whole. The mystical aspect of life would open, and
spiritual power would become real. Essentially, a
lifelong friendship would begin to develop with the
Spirit of the universe.

Native Americans believed that Spirit often took
the form of an animal, so they became sensitive to
their surroundings. In addition, it was believed that
the individual would be guided to make an amulet
or something to be worn which would remind the
person of the vision and the gift of revelation
received.

Many cultures throughout the world have practices that help a child become an adult and become

aware of the mystical dimension of life. Our culture is currently devoid of such rites of passage. Our idea of becoming an adult is that of acquiring a driver's license. This binds us to our world rather than helping us discover the hidden and mysterious aspects of life. We often take our children to Sunday school to learn about God, but in most cases there is no opportunity for personal reflection and an experience of the Presence.

However, it is not ritual we need, although rites of passage that are relevant to the third millennium can be conceived. We need quiet and solitude, so the voice still and small can reveal to us what lies beyond our five senses and even the faculties of thought, feeling, and imagination. We live on the earth, but our universe is more than stars, galaxies, and cosmic dust. Within us are cosmic forces beyond imagining. It is strange, but these forces are destined to course through our being. This is the heart and core of our purpose.

An Invitation

Emmanuel means "God is with us," but people go to the grave never knowing or feeling the Presence. The joy of conscious union is unrealized, and therefore life has never really been lived. Air has been inhaled and exhaled, children may have been conceived and birthed, but we were never really

born. We never knew our purpose, and therefore
we never received our mission, our call within a
call. Let us take conscious and deliberate steps to
be fully alive, to experience our purpose, and to
receive our God-mission.

As part of our willingness to allow cosmic forces
to express themselves through us, let us embark
upon a vision quest. God is calling us. Solitude,
stillness, and silence summon us, and the time has
come to heed the invitation. We will give the gift of
our attention to Spirit and receive the gifts of revelation and mission.

Revelation can occur at any time, even when we
are in the midst of difficult circumstances. New insight often comes like a friend who stands with us
or holds us when we hurt and are in pain. However,
divine friendship does not fully unfold until we turn
Godward as a natural part of our lives, rather than
solely as an attempt to have the One help us
through some challenging situation.

Set aside a time when you can "come . . . apart
. . . a while." For tens of thousands of years, seekers have done this. They have responded to what
they felt inside. At the deepest level, it is not a vision
or phenomenon that they sought, although either
may come. People wanted to know that their lives
had meaning, that they could make a difference,

that they came into the world for a reason. They wanted to know why they were here.

Those upon the quest yearn for mission, but intuitively they know it is not of this world. Mission is not a human thing. It is a divine gift that comes as the result of knowing the Creator. Therefore, the retreat into solitude becomes the beginning of a lifelong relationship with the Presence.

This is the way it is with human relationships. We spend an evening with someone, and it is a "vision of joy," but our destiny is more than a singular experience; it is a shared life with another. I believe it is to be this way with Spirit. In fact, our friendship with the One will eventually meld into a oneness that is beyond the scope of this book.

Let there be specific ingredients to your quest for meaning and mission. First, feel the anticipation of a spiritual orphan who will meet and greet its Creator. Sense the gathering of spiritual forces. Call them forth with thanksgiving. Be willing to feel as you have never felt before. Open your mind to the absurd. Consider that there is mystery behind all form and that, moment by moment, it will make itself known to you.

Begin to determine how you will say no to your world. It continually demands your attention, but now your senses and faculties of thinking, feeling, and imagination are turning to Spirit. Your motive, your intent, is being purified and lifted up.

When you "come . . . apart . . . a while," take no books or tapes with you. At this important time in your life, your thoughts are more important than the insights of the most illumined people on earth. This is a time for listening for *inner* voices. As you will discover, some are your own, but one is the voice of God, which illumines and stirs you to new heights.

As you put aside the world for a time, you will discover an inner kingdom. Residing there are parts of you that you had forgotten, had never wanted to know, or had never gotten to know. During this quest, you will face yourself and your foibles, and this courageous act is prelude to the discovery of your true self.

It was this way for Native Americans. They placed themselves in the quiet and silently faced their fears and sense of inadequacy. These two became their friends, because they helped to produce a humble spirit that "called" to the Great Spirit who had called the person to the wilderness. The humble one became exalted!

The quest for meaning passes through this seeming valley, for we face parts of ourselves we have tried to cover up. This is why we shy away from solitude, stillness, and silence. We hear what we have not wanted to hear. We discover what we have covered. And besides, the busy mind believes solitude, stillness, and silence are silly. They are fruitless. "Don't just sit there; do something," the worldly mind declares, while the mind of God answers, "Don't just do something; sit there."

The interesting thing is that just sitting there accomplishes something that we cannot achieve by ourselves. Solitude, reflection, and listening give Spirit an opportunity to do Its work. We become clay in the potter's hand, rather than anguishing in an attempt to mold ourselves into something acceptable to the world. Our receptivity allows the Master to make a masterpiece that is of value to the world.

Jesus spent time in the wilderness. He faced himself and, with his Father's help, overcame the inner voices and temptations that befell him. He received his mission and promptly began his ministry. This is always the story after the human self is faced. A purpose-filled being with a mission emerges from the silence and takes its rightful place in the world.

Spiritual Mentor

I trust that you will pursue a vision quest, for not only does it bear much fruit, but it also introduces you to a way of life which allows spiritual forces to be expressed in and through and as you. This is a path you will walk alone, but remember, there are many who have gone before you. Native American children withdrew into the wilderness so they could become aware of the spiritual dimension of life.

As a child, your life was a mystery and an adventure. Everything was fresh and new. Perhaps you lost your curious self as you grew older. Now is the time to return to the purity of the past, when your curious nature ruled the day. Once, you uncovered the mystery of your outer world. Now another unknown region awaits you. May you respond to the willingness of your curious self to explore the inner world that rests within you.

It is not necessary, but often it is helpful, to enlist the support of a spiritual friend as you embark upon your quest for meaning. This individual can support you as you prepare to "come . . . apart . . . a while" and can be an accepting, listening ear when you return from the wilderness. There will be joys to share, because there will be more clarity in your life, but there will also be much that has emerged which you will need to reflect upon. The answers and conclusions are for you and you alone to discover, but a spiritual mentor can assist you in finding your way.

Your spiritual mentor need not be someone with all the answers. In fact, this friend should have more questions than answers. However, the questions will help you find answers and unearth the Truth. The spiritual mentor should appreciate mystery and not want to strip it away. He or she should value silence and feel privileged to share this adventure with you.

Through the ages, spiritual traditions have seen the value of periods of silence, prayer, and meditation. In the Christian tradition, many people have taken to heart Jesus' suggestion that they "come . . . apart . . . a while." Dear friend, this is what I am suggesting. As long as there have been people who went to the wilderness to find the wellspring of living water, there have been spiritual friends or mentors who helped the seekers not only prepare for the quest, but also to garner as much as possible from their time alone with God.

The Giving of Gifts

In all grand happenings, something is given, but it is also true to say that something is given up. We know our purpose—to know God, to experience the Presence. We stand with outstretched arms toward the One, but then a question is asked of us, "What are you willing to give up?" Intuitively, we know what stands between us and an experience of the Presence. It may be unforgiveness, false pride, the need to be a doer, fear of solitude, or some other such motivation.

You see, the discovery of purpose and mission is a shared giving. We give up what stands as a barrier to our making a difference in the world, and then we receive the gift of mission. This is why it is said that a spiritual life is not an adding to, but a letting go.

We are spiritual beings engineered for revelation and for God's work. In Truth, spiritual awakening is more than part of the divine plan; it is its first step. This is the way it was for Mother Teresa and Dr. Schweitzer.

They were called to purpose just as we are. They responded, and they received a call within a call—a mission given to them by God. Mother Teresa's mission was to be love in action. Her call within a call was to minister to the poorest of the poor. Schweitzer's mission was an expression of reverence for life, and he fulfilled his mission as he cared for the sick in Africa. These missions are worthy of any human being.

Leaven for One's Life

Can you see that our quest for meaning reduces life to its base elements? First, there is the need to experience the One who created us. Out of this experience comes our mission. This is alchemy in that clichés like *love one another, care for the sick, revere all life* take on immense meaning and become a driving force in our lives. What makes them more than words is that they have been revealed to us by Spirit.

The result is that we carry in our minds and hearts a few simple words which are leaven for our lives. Do you remember Jesus' parable about the small portion of yeast or leaven that permeates the whole loaf of bread? Purpose and mission expand and touch all aspects of our lives. They are leaven for our lives.

A Going In, a Coming Out

By heeding the call to experience the Presence, we receive our mission. If the call to purpose is a going in, our mission is a coming out. Spirit calls us to Itself, and we journey within. We touch the Divine, and a stargate forms through which Spirit may express Itself. This expression becomes our mission. It is Spirit's journeying out into our lives and the world. This is God's plan.

Please know that while our work can be our mission, our mission cannot be our work. We can retire from our work, but not our mission. It leavens our life always. Like our purpose of knowing God, our mission is always with us. Did Mother Teresa ever cease being love in action? Did Albert Schweitzer ever stop revering life?

Your mission must have this same enduring quality. It will come to you during your vision quest in a time of reflection or when you least expect it, but it will come. Your intent to be of service and your willingness to face your humanity and give up the barriers that stand between you and an experience of the Presence will, through grace, give birth to your call within a call—your mission.

Mile Markers

- Everyone has a mission.
- Cosmic forces are destined to course through us and into the world.
- Solitude, stillness, and silence provide Spirit an opportunity to touch and transform our consciousness.
- Purpose is a going in; mission is a coming out.

Adventure Two

A Call Within a Call

This is the true joy in life, the being used for a purpose recognized by yourself as a mighty one.

—George Bernard Shaw

Do you remember the television program *Mission Impossible*? Every episode began with a proposed mission and the statement "should you decide to accept it." Each person is given a mission and the freedom to either accept or reject it. It may take years for us to prepare ourselves so that we can learn of our mission or fulfill it.

If you have not yet discovered your God-mission, the time is drawing near or you would not be studying *The Quest for Meaning*. When you have a sense of what lies before you, do not be concerned if it appears you lack the skills necessary to do what is yours to do. Moses was given the great commission of leading the Hebrews out of Egypt toward the Promised Land. When he received his mission, he balked and told God that he was not qualified: "I

42

am not eloquent . . . I am slow of speech and of tongue" (Ex. 4:10).

Many of us would answer in a similar way, but the wonder of mission is that as we take the first step, gifts, talents, and resources necessary to fulfill the mission show themselves, often for the first time. So plunge ahead, dear friend; you have purpose, and now you are ready to receive your God-mission.

Soul-Talk

 God is calling me. Slowly write this three times. Repeat it aloud or silently each day during this Adventure.

1. _____

2. _____

3. _____

Soul-Thoughts

After you have contemplated this declaration, write down your thoughts.

1. *Do you know your mission? If you do, what is it?*

Where will you go? (Please insure that the place is secluded and simple in its amenities.) Even if you think you know your mission, and certainly if you do not, prepare for a personal vision quest.

When will you go?

What are you willing to cease doing during this time of seeking and silence? (This practice strengthens the no-saying power of the mind and helps you discover what stands between you and your mission.)

2. Please consider the following guidelines and helps for your vision-quest experience.

- As you travel to your vision-quest site, have no distractions. Do not listen to the radio or read. Instead, turn your attention to Spirit.

- While you are on your vision quest, do not read or listen to tapes or anything that ties you to the world. This is an *inner* journey. Take a small paper pad with you and a pen to record any thoughts or experiences that come to you.

- Upon your arrival, write a dedication statement that tells why you have gone on this spiritual pilgrimage.

- Accept your wandering mind and any feelings, thoughts, or images that rise up within you. This is a time of non-resistance. Rest gently with this idea: *I resist not. I embrace all experiences in my outer world and my inner world.*

- See all that you see, hear, smell, feel, taste as an expression of the One. In this way, sacredness will surround and enfold you.

- Listen . . . for even the animals and the wind will speak to you.

Turn the corner of this page, so you can return to it easily. *After your vision quest, please record a summary of your experience below.*

My Vision Quest

Off the Main Trail

Reflect on Jesus in the wilderness and his three temptations (Mt. 4:1–11). During this time, Jesus faced himself. It is said that his temptations are also ours. Accept this premise for the purpose of contemplation and explore the possibility that you have faced these choices as well. *What were each of Jesus' temptations? How are they yours? How can Jesus' experience help you when you are tempted again?*

Stepping-Stone

If you have struggled in an attempt to discover your God-mission, something is standing between you and this experience. In most instances, nothing needs to be added to an individual. Something needs to be released. *What is it that you need to let go of in order to continue your spiritual unfoldment?*

God is calling me.

Chapter Three

The Greater Circle

Mission can be described in many ways—to care for the poorest of the poor, to heal the sick, to feed the hungry, to clothe the naked, to see in others something they cannot see in themselves, to help children find and express their gifts and talents, to teach and live the Truth, to bring hope and encouragement to the downtrodden, and to revere all life. The words that describe mission are endless, but not as enduring and eternal as the greater circle, called "love," which can be drawn around the many words.

Our purpose is to know God, and when we are upon this path, our mission appears. It is that we are to "love one another." This was Jesus' great and only commandment. He commanded cosmic forces and could have demanded that we do many things, but he called us to love. He asked that we draw the greater circle and let it encompass everything we do. Thus, knowing God and loving are joined. "He who does not love does not know God; for God is love" (1 Jn. 4:8).

No book on the quest for meaning could be complete without a chapter on love, for every spiritual way of life flows from the heart of God. Every religion declares that a life of love is the answer.

Love is what we sense in the midst of us. It is as present as the human heart we feel beating in our chests. Love is the common thread that binds us one to another. We will be our best and know the Truth about one another when our mission is love.

The Sacred Clay

If our mission is a pottery bowl filled with care and compassion and offered to humankind, love is the unformed clay out of which the earthen vessel is made. When we give ourselves to an experience of the Presence, we discover not only that God is love, but that we are love as well. Some say we were made of the dust of the earth. True, our bodies are composed of elements and compounds found on our planet, but we are not made of dust. We are made of love. Spirit reached into Itself, into Its heart, and made us.

As your mission begins to take shape, do not forget the nature of the unformed clay that is molded and fired, for mission is never about an individual. It is not for the one; it is for the many. Because love is the essence of mission, mission always includes others.

We do not eat from the earthen bowl and bring care and compassion to our lips. We offer it to those with whom we share life, and in this way we are cared for and shown compassion. To feed another is to feed ourselves. To teach another is to learn. We are mystically joined to one another. We may stand beside one another like trees in a forest, but our roots are intertwined, and we draw nourishment from the same earth below and sky above.

We Are Not Many

Mission eventually brings us into a mystical teaching of Jesus. "'I was hungry and you gave me food, I was thirsty and you gave me drink, I was a stranger and you welcomed me, I was naked and you clothed me, I was sick and you visited me, I was in prison and you came to me.' 'Truly, I say to you, as you did it to one of the least of these my brethren, you did it to me'" (Mt. 25:35–36, 40). Mission makes oneness practical and makes it clear that we are in this together. To turn our backs upon anyone is to turn from a part of ourselves. Through mission, we experience oneness with one another.

The Center of the Circle

There are many things that a human being can do, and we will discuss them in the chapter on work, but unless our work is birthed by love, what we do is drudgery. It exhausts us and is a hiding place, rather than a place of discovery. When our work is labor, who we are remains hidden. The true Self is never seen. However, when our mission is love, regardless of our work, we are placed at the center of the greater circle, where we discover our true nature.

Some people insist that our nature is sinful, but this is not true. We are made in Love's image, and no atrocity can change the Truth of our being. An evil deed, like work without love, only hides the Truth of what we are.

Remember when we were children and felt hurt? How comforting it was to take hold of our favorite stuffed animal or doll and squeeze it tight. To this inanimate object, we shed our tears and professed our love. And amazingly, we felt better. In some instances, we even felt loved! How could this be? Wasn't our companion lifeless and filled with stuffing? There was no heart beating in the doll or animal we hugged. But it seemed as though it were loving us.

Where did the love come from? It came from within us. We were feeling hurt, but we reached out and loved, and love revealed itself. Our true nature emerged from within us. In that moment, we were true to what we are.

Our mission grants us the same gift. When we remember that love is the unformed clay which gives form to the pottery bowl we will offer to the human family, we come alive. We know ourselves as never before. What we learned from our time as children when we felt hurt and alone can now serve as a foundation of our mission. To express love is to *experience* love.

Mission Messages

Every human being who comes to know God receives four messages. Each one of them is profound and life-changing, but not because of the words. It is the experience of the Presence that shatters the previous life of loneliness and pain and points the way to a new beginning. Nevertheless, each message becomes part of the person's mission, and the message shared is multiplied as it spreads from person to person. The messages are the heart and soul of mission. They form the greater circle that encompasses everything we do.

The *first message* is, "Lo, I am with you always" (Mt. 28:20). This statement made by Jesus as he departed from his disciples is conveyed by God to every human being. Perhaps not with words, but in Spirit's way, it becomes clear; we are not alone.

In 1934 while at Ross Barrier, Little America, South Pole, Admiral Richard E. Byrd sensed God's

love. Admiral Byrd was collecting scientific data
and, as it turned out, data about humanity. He
stood outside, more utterly alone than all but a few
of us ever are, and he wrote that he felt a rhythm,
a warmth—standing in the coldest cold on earth—
which went to the heart of man's despair and found
it groundless.

This is a message we are called to share. It is part
of our mission no matter what we do. I recall a
story about a chaplain who accompanied a combat
unit during the Vietnam War. On one sortie, the
platoon was pinned down by enemy fire for hours.
The minister crawled from foxhole to foxhole to be
with the men. One soldier said, "Why are you
here?" The chaplain answered, "Because *you* are."
That's mission, because it is love in action.

The *second message* we receive is that we are
God's beloved. In John's first letter, he calls those to
whom he is writing "beloved." When Jesus was
baptized he heard the same message: "This is my
beloved Son" (Mt. 3:17). This is true of each of us in
spite of what we have done or not done or what has
been done to us. God's nature is love, and we are
going to be loved and cherished whether we believe we deserve it or not!

I remember counseling with a woman who
wanted to find love in the arms of a man. It was important to her that she be married. She felt a void

inside that she believed could be filled only through marriage. I suggested that she first find God. "If you do," I said, "you will find love." I still recall the day she spoke with me after a church service with tears in her eyes and said, "I know God loves me." She had had an experience of the Presence in which she sensed she, too, was God's beloved. This experience awaits us all, and it is also one of the mission messages we are to share with the world.

The *third* and *fourth messages* are akin to one another. The third was expressed by Jesus when he addressed the woman caught in adultery. She feared for her life, for the punishment for adultery was death, and the men who brought her to Jesus were prepared to carry out the sentence. Trembling and weeping, she covered herself at Jesus' feet. The men asked him, "What do you say about her?" (Jn. 8:5) Jesus stooped down, wrote in the sand and said, "Let him who is without sin among you be the first to throw a stone at her" (Jn. 8:7). Slowly the men tossed their stones aside and walked away. Jesus turned his attention to the woman: "'Woman, where are they? Has no one condemned you?' She said, 'No one, Lord.' And Jesus said, 'Neither do I condemn you; go, and do not sin again'" (Jn. 8:10–11).

Love does not condemn. We are always loved and cherished, but many of us do not feel it because of guilt and self-condemnation. Rather than assisting others in releasing condemnation, we sometimes reinforce it; however, when love is our mission, condemnation falls away. We may suggest to others that they cease their debilitating behavior, as Jesus did to the woman, "Go, and do not sin again," but we declare no one guilty. In fact, love goes the extra mile, for it does not demand that people act in a certain way. This brings us to the *fourth message.*

When love is our mission, we cease trying to fix people. The old mission of trying to repair others, ourselves, and the world is no more. Love does not aspire to perform maintenance upon those who appear broken. Instead, love says, *"I accept you just the way you are."*

Acceptance will show us another world and help create a guilt- and condemnation-free atmosphere where people can find themselves. There is no need to be defensive, for no one is holding limiting thoughts about anyone. Acceptance is one of the most wonderful gifts we can share with the human family, but before it becomes a mission-message we share with the world, we must accept ourselves as we are.

Practical, Yet Mystical

Those whose mission is love eventually experience a mystical oneness with God, other people, and the world. From this mountaintop experience, creation is viewed from a divine perspective. There is a tendency to want to remain on the summit, but love was never meant solely for the high places. The valley calls, for the need for love is where most of us live. We must return to the valley—to our family, friends, strangers, and our place of work. This is where love is put into practice.

This is why the family is so important, for there is no more challenging or, hopefully, more supportive environment in which to love one another. Our place of work is another opportunity to practice loving. It may seem like work is about tasks, filling orders, making money, producing products, and providing services, but the real issue is getting along with our co-workers. We all have "people" jobs; even the writer who works in isolation must hold in mind the reader, so that what is written is relevant.

Those people who have been most true to the mission of loving seem so far ahead of us. They feel a part of us, and we feel separate from them. They have found something we don't even know is available to us. Fear and separation dominate our lives, while oneness and love are a part of their daily experience. This is why they return to us. Oneness teaches them that they cannot go on into the infinite greater circle of love without us. They say, "I cannot go on without you, for you are a part of me." So they return to the valley where we struggle with life—not to fix us, but to accept us as we are.

The Circle That Never Ends

Just as our purpose of knowing God is always before us, so it is with our mission of loving one another. "Love one another" is an eternal call whether we are saint or sinner. The only difference is that the saint has responded to the call to love one another and stands in the center of the greater circle. All others think they stand outside the circle, but even now it is expanding to encircle them, for none is free until *all* are free.

Mile Markers

- Mission is never solely for the one; it is for the many.
- Our mission is to love one another.
- Mission makes oneness practical.
- We are not alone.
- We are God's beloved.
- We are not condemned.
- God accepts us just the way we are.

Adventure Three

The Greater Circle

Love one another.

—Jesus

What you do is not as important as the spirit from which it is done. For instance, you can perform your job because you need the money and must make ends meet, or you can work because you want to make a difference in the world and people's lives.

I have had the wonderful experience of ordaining a few ministers in their churches, with their congregations sharing the reverence and revelry of the ordination service. In every instance, we opened ourselves to a consciousness of love before the minister was ordained. The conferring of ordination was not as important as the consciousness out of which it was done.

As you continue your quest for meaning and search for mission, pause and ponder the following meditation. Read the words in mind or out loud, but be sure to rest with each line. Let the voice still and small speak to you. Then continue with this adventure on the quest.

The Sacred Clay Meditation

My mission is a simple pottery bowl
   Made of the ground of being,
   Its shape receptive,
   Willing to receive
   What comes from above,
   What comes from within—

An earthen vessel filled with what the earth needs:
   Compassion and care,
   Peace and power,
   Joy and kindness.

Formed of clay.
   By another name,
   It's love.
   The ground I walk on—
   Once mountains high,
   Now humbled and brought low—
   Such is love's way.

Love shaped by unseen hands
   To form the sacred bowl
   Offered to all.

Take what it holds:
  Compassion and care,
  Peace and power,
  Joy and kindness—

And take the bowl as well,
For the sacred clay is love.

Soul-Talk

I live at the heart of the greater circle.
Write this three times and repeat each
day during this Adventure.

1. _____

2. _____

3. _____

Soul-Thoughts

After contemplation, write down your
thoughts.

In a ministry I served, we used to pass a small stuffed replica of the earth called a "hug-a-planet" throughout the congregation during the service, so the people could give it a hug. There is something wonderful about this simple practice. The people enjoyed it, not because they received something from the globe, but because they gave themselves the gift of love.

1. Either in the privacy of your home or as part of a class, hug a stuffed animal. *What do you feel? Did it come from the inanimate object?*

After this exercise, reflect upon the idea that what we want to experience, we must express. A scientist might write this insight as a formula: experience = expression. *Is this accurate? Write your thoughts below.*

2. From your own experience or from a book you have read or story you have heard, recall a person who experienced divine love. *Please share your experience or the story you heard.*

3. *If you have not experienced God's love, what will you do to prepare yourself for this experience?* Remember, experience = expression.

4. Read the story of Jesus responding to the woman caught in adultery. *Why did Jesus bend down and write in the sand when he spoke to the men who wanted to stone the woman? Would this be helpful to you if you faced a hostile individual? How would you "bend down" in such a situation?*

What do you think Jesus wrote in the sand?

Why was Jesus' statement, "Neither do I condemn you," so freeing to the woman?

Off the Main Trail

 For the next seven days, ponder Jesus' statement, "Lo, I am with you always." Become sensitive to your surroundings and to your innermost being, for God is closer than hands and feet and breathing. How does it feel?

Stepping-Stone

 Select one of the three remaining mission messages and share it with the world this week. In the next two weeks, share the remaining messages. Remember, actions speak louder than words. *What did you do?*

I live at the heart of the greater circle.

Chapter Four

1 Feel God's Pleasure

The Academy Award-winning picture *Chariots of Fire* records the struggles and triumphs of two British Olympians prior to and during the 1924 games. Eric Liddell and Harold Abraham are sprinters initially in competition with one another. Mr. Liddell is a Christian who has felt the call to be a missionary in China. He and his sister Jeannie are to minister together, but the games intervene.

Jeannie wants her brother to forego the Olympic competition and accompany her to China. Eric is called to go, but he knows he must first run in the games. When they discuss the matter, Eric says to his sister: "I believe God made me for a purpose. . . . He also made me fast, and when I run, I feel His pleasure. To give it up would be to hold Him in contempt. To win is to honor Him."

Years ago when I saw this movie, I was struck by the statement, "When I run, I feel His pleasure." I never forgot the phrase. Surely, when we share our special gifts, talents, and skills, we feel God's pleasure.

Giving a Gift of Ourselves

A life of meaning is also a life of joy. It comes not because we receive something for ourselves, but because we *give* something of ourselves. Many of us believe that happiness comes when we receive accolades or when desired things happen to us. Admittedly, there is delight when life treats us well, but the boundless joy of God is ours when we uncover and then share our special gifts with the world.

I believe every person has a God-given gift or talent. Some express gifts that are athletic or artistic in nature. Other people inspire those around them through hard work, persistence, kindness, or selflessness. Regardless of the gift, happiness comes when our special skill is discovered and used for God's glory and as a blessing to all. Just as Eric Liddell felt God's pleasure when he ran, so we will experience joy when we share our talent with humanity.

The Divine Intent

It is not enough that God *is;* the divine plan demands that God become or come into expression. Within our Creator are myriad possibilities, but this is not enough. The possibilities must come into being.

Through the ages, the divine intent has been expressed in many ways: "Let your light so shine" (Mt. 5:16) or "I have come into the world, to bear witness to the truth" (Jn. 18:37). In the quietness of our souls and as the desires of our hearts, we sense the divine intent. Spirit is saying to each of us, *"I am in you. I am the Truth of your being. Bear witness to this Truth; bear witness to Me. I am the light of the world. Let the light shine. I am, have always been, and always shall be, but let Me come into your life and into the world. I seek expression in and through and as you. I am, but it is part of my plan that I be made manifest. I am the formless, seeking form. I need a door through which to enter. You have been created to be this door."*

It is not enough that each of us is made in God's image and likeness. That which is hidden must be revealed. The unseen Presence desires to show Itself in the world. It is not enough that we are spiritual beings; we must *live* as beings of Spirit. It is not enough that we have the capacity to be compassionate. We must *be* compassionate. It is not enough that we can love unconditionally. We will never be fully alive and experience the fullness of our oneness with all life until we live lives of love. Always and forevermore, we feel the divine intent. Spirit is seeking expression, and we will know that what poet Robert Browning called "the imprisoned splendor" is being released from bondage when we share our gifts and feel God's pleasure.

Spiritual Gifts

In Paul's first letter to the Corinthians, he writes of spiritual gifts and their purpose: "To each is given the manifestation of the Spirit for the common good" (1 Cor. 12:7). Nine different gifts were being shared in the community. They ranged from healing to speaking in tongues: "All these are inspired by one and the same Spirit who apportions to each one individually" (1 Cor. 12:11).

I have said that the divine intent is expression. Paul speaks of the manifestation of the Spirit. It may be hard to believe that we have been created for this purpose, but we have. God's expression and our joy are eternally bound together. Let us never forget that our Creator is the Spirit of the universe. Appearances and our behavior may declare otherwise, but we are spiritual beings conceived for a divine purpose.

Gifts, talents, and abilities vary from person to person. Athletes have many different skills. Some run like the wind. Others swim. Some can hit a baseball; others, a golf ball. In our society, athletic skills open doors to fame and financial wealth. Discipline is learned, and persistence practiced. These are life skills and will come into play even when the

·athlete is retired. However, as Eric Liddell said, the purpose of expressing these skills is to honor the One who provided them.

No matter what our gift, let us realize its origin and that it was provided as an avenue for Spirit's expression. Society delights in witnessing the gifts of dancers, artists, musicians, and so on, but these gifted ones can teach us about values and the importance of contributing to the lives of others. Many gifted people realize this and, because of their public prominence, are able to bring a message of hope to thousands. For instance, a bedside visit by a favorite baseball player to a sick child can bolster the little one's desire to live and excel. A concert violinist's performance at a school of music can inspire a renewed dedication in the students as they set their sights on playing their instruments with passion.

Most of us do not live public lives observed by the masses, but those around us watch the way we live. We have the potential to be a force for good. When we express our talents, they are witnessed and therefore can serve for the "common good."

Uncovering Your Gift

Dear friend, you have a singular purpose—to know God, to discover what you are. It is a shared purpose, for it is my purpose too. You have a mission. It can be described in many ways, but the simplest is "love." You are to live your life as if you were united with everyone and everything, because you are. You are to be a blessing to this world, and because of the life you live, you will be blessed. I have the same mission and quest.

To assist you in living and enable you to fulfill your mission, you have been given a gift. If you have not yet found your gift, now is the time to begin to seek it earnestly. Not only will you find happiness and joy in sharing your gift, but your Creator will find an avenue of expression into the world.

The search for your gift begins with humility. Please realize that it is not solely yours or for you alone. It is something Spirit has given to you with the hope that one day you will return it to the Giver. On that day, your gift will be a blessing to the human family.

Perhaps you are adamant in believing that you have no special talent. Even this attitude of "not me" is favorable, for it is a form of humility. Our wise God has created the world in such a way that the humble will be exalted. The divine law of humility will lift you up.

Through the course of your life, many "hints" have been given about your talent or skill. What can you do and lose all sense of time in the doing?

For me it is writing. I can begin to write late in the evening and fail to realize that the sun is rising. What have you wanted to do since you were a child? Maybe you were encouraged to put aside this foolish dream, because people said no one makes a decent living doing that! Now is the time to dream again.

When are you most joyful? Do you enjoy being with people or are you most at ease when you are alone? What are your current hobbies? Perhaps they tell you of the natural inclinations that Spirit has planted like a seed within you. Do you receive your greatest sense of accomplishment in helping others? What could you be happy doing all day?

Questions such as these loosen the soil of our souls, so seeds planted long ago can sprout and grow. Once, a woman told me that her life was changed when she heard a minister talk about hidden talents. She recalled how much she enjoyed painting, even though she had not lifted a brush for years. When she returned home, she took out her art supplies and began to paint. Today, watercolor is an important part of her life; she experiences joy in losing herself in painting, and others experience beauty because of her special gift.

I suspect this story can be repeated again and again. Of course, *many* of us have not developed the talents that rest within us, but we can begin. It is never too late. ·

Elizabeth Layton discovered her talent when she was 68 years old. She was prone to depression, but found freedom in drawing and painting. Her first efforts at art opened a door to a unique creativity that has been praised by Kay Larson in a 1983 review published in *New York* magazine: "Considering her background, I am tempted to call Layton a genius." You may not be called a genius, but the special gift is there. It is never too late to feel God's pleasure.

Please realize that not all of us will uncover an artistic talent which brings fame and fortune. Some of us just need another outlook on life. We need to give ourselves to something with abandon. It was this way with Elizabeth Layton, for her thirty years of depression lifted as she gave herself to art.

For us, we need to do a new thing. Commitment and dedication to developing skills and spiritual values bring us one step closer to feeling God's pleasure.

Forsaking Your Gift

We have a gift, but it can remain hidden and dormant all our lives. Remember, the gift is an avenue of Spirit's expression, and when we say no to the gift, we say no to God and to our joy. Many a special talent has atrophied because of the need to make ends meet.

It is a question of values. So often making a living supercedes making a contribution to the world. Fear and insecurity are the true culprits in this instance. We fail to realize that Spirit's expression not only blesses us, but it also blesses the world. When we experience God's pleasure our consciousness of joy banishes fear and insecurity. With these impostors gone, ideas can flow and opportunities are recognized. Joy makes us bold and able to take steps we were reluctant to take before.

If we have not developed our gift since childhood, its unfoldment now may mean starting over. This does not mean our life has been pointless, but only that we have a wealth of experience to bring to bear in the quest of honoring the Presence.

Prior to the 1996 Olympics in Atlanta, I heard a story of a woman who earned a six-figure income in international business, but she gave it up to ride a bicycle. It seems absurd, but her story was an inspiration to those who are tempted to be "foolish." I don't know how skillful she was as a racer, but as a liver of life, she was a champion. You see, it is not always about winning, for being number one is a human dream. The key is attunement to the divine intent. This oneness allows the divine message to be given. In the case of the Olympic cyclist, the message is not to abandon our jobs and ride into the sunset; it is to have the courage to follow an inner voice.

The Gift of Those in Need

Perhaps you persist in insisting that you have no special gift or skill. Or maybe you are thinking about those people who are handicapped or born with disabilities. What gifts do *they* have? How can someone lying comatose in a hospital become an avenue of God's expression?

The Truth is that people who appear to have little or are unable to speak or move have a *great* gift to give. Their gift is their need. Wherever there is a need—a person lying comatose in the hospital or those dying of famine in distant lands—a gift is being given that calls us to compassion and asks us to help. The tragedy is that we often fail to realize the wonder of this gift. We lose an opportunity for the Presence to be made manifest as love and caring. However, when we receive the gift of need and answer with compassion, soothing words, and helpful actions, the divine intent is fulfilled. God's joy is evident, people are helped, the human family is more unified and feels once more the thrill of the expression of God's presence.

The Truth is that through the course of our lives we share the gift of need with others. Sometimes it is recognized and other times it is not. However, even if our need goes unfulfilled, let us not become callous to the needs that are presented to us, for the hand which reaches out to us is the hand of God. It is saying: *"Receive this precious gift by sharing your heart and your own special gift with Me. I offer you not only a need and an opportunity, I offer you joy, for when I am released from within you, you feel My pleasure!"*

Mile Markers

- A life of meaning comes not because we receive something for ourselves, but because we *give* something of ourselves.
- Each of us has a gift to give.
- We experience joy when we give our talent to humanity.
- Spirit is seeking expression, for the divine intent *is* expression.
- The gift some people give is their need.

Adventure Four

1 Feel God's Pleasure

A talent is formed in stillness.
—Johann Wolfgang Goethe

The giving of gifts is an art. We can be like the business executive who asks his secretary to buy his wife a birthday present, or we can search for the perfect gift ourselves. However, those who make gift giving an art give of themselves. This is why children are so joyful when they give a gift to their parents that they have made with their own hands.

Our God knows the art of giving, for Spirit has given Itself to us. There is the gift of life and the gift of love. Spirit has made us a part of everything, because the Presence pervades not only the planet and everything on it, but the cosmos. And there is more. Spirit has given Itself not only to us; through our gifts and talents, Spirit continues to give Itself to others and to the creation. It is for this reason that we are called to be givers—to give presents and praise to one another, but also to let the Presence give the gifts *It* would give.

Soul-Talk

I give my gift to the world.
Write this three times and repeat each
day during this Adventure.

1. _____

2. _____

3. _____

Soul-Thoughts

After contemplation, write down your
thoughts.

*1. Are you aware of your spiritual gift?
If you are, what is it?*

Declare it to be a manifestation of
Spirit given for the common good.

2. If you are not aware of your spiritual gift or if you sense there is more that you can give the world, ponder the following questions. You read many of these questions in this chapter, but now it is time to answer them.

What are you doing when you feel God's pleasure?

What are you doing when you lose all sense of time?

What did you dream of doing when you were a child?

What did you dream of being when you were a child?

Are you currently fulfilling these dreams?

What would you do if you could do anything?

What gifts are required to do this thing?

What are your hobbies?

What is happening when you experience pure fun?

If you were a teacher, what would you teach?

Please reflect upon your answers to these questions. Think of them as arrows pointing to your special gift and talent. Let the following question be a seed that grows into your full realization that you can make a difference: *What is it that you have to share with the world?*

Off the Main Trail

It is often inspirational to read about or talk with people who consciously know their gift and share it with the world. Do research and find someone who gave up a "successful" job in order to pursue and express a special gift.

Stepping-Stone

 Be alert this week to the needs that are presented to you. Transform your view of them. They are not needs; they are gifts. *What was presented to you? Were you able to receive it?*

I give my gift to the world.

Chapter Five

Sacred Work

The Family Business

"What do you do?" "What business are you in?" "What's your job?" These questions are repeated daily by strangers making small talk on airplanes as they fly home after a day of conducting business. A dialogue often begins between these travelers. Career paths are discussed. Business contacts are sometimes made, but primarily two individuals have passed the time with one another. Most likely, they part never to meet again.

Children never play the "What do you do?" game, for in our society, children play and adults work. However, Jesus at age twelve told his parents that he was about his Father's business. (And it wasn't carpentry.) "His parents went to Jerusalem every year at the Feast of the Passover. And when He was twelve years old, they went up to Jerusalem according to the custom of the Feast. When they had finished the days, as they returned, the Boy Jesus lingered behind in Jerusalem . . . Now so it was *that* after three days they found Him in the temple, sitting in the midst of the teachers, both listening to them and asking them questions. And all who heard Him were astonished at His understanding and answers . . . His mother said to Him, 'Son why have You done this to us? Look, Your father and I have sought You anxiously.' And He said to them, 'Why did you seek Me? Did you not know I must be about My Father's business?'" (Lk. 2:41–43, 46–50 NKJV)

It is difficult to determine the nature of the Father's work by reading the description of this episode in the Master's life. Jesus, the boy, was listening to the learned scholars of the temple. He asked them questions and dialogued with them. This reinforces the human tendency to assume that God's work is religious. However, it is possible for a minister to fail to conduct the Father's business, while a prison guard may be gainfully "employed" by Spirit.

Some of us work for family businesses. In fact, most corporations were initially family-owned and family-run business ventures. The experience of the corner lemonade stand evolves until it becomes a restaurant or a computer-manufacturing plant. The possibilities are immense, for employment takes many forms. Some of us labor with our hands; others with our minds. Farmers work the earth; teachers sow seeds in the minds of children.

Some people build things; others buy and sell what is built.

In the years to come, our children will be employed in jobs that do not even exist today. For instance, when I was a child there were no astronauts or personal computers. The industries that support the space program and personal computing now employ hundreds of thousands of people. Even our nation's space program can trace its roots to the Wright brothers, who took flight on the dunes of Kitty Hawk, North Carolina.

But all of us are part of the family of humanity. Its roots are in Spirit, and our Creator has work for us to do. Apparently, even twelve-year-olds are called to serve in this "business." There is meaning in this call, and it births a hope that everyone can make a contribution to the divine work.

A Storefront for God

I have a friend who is an associate in God's work. He buys and sells used furniture, but his vision is much greater than what he does. He says that his store is a front for God. One day a young family came to his storefront in search of furniture for their home. Not only did my friend sell them furnishing at a reasonable price, but he also helped them move it into their house. He made the sale, but he also made new friends, and the family will probably always remember the man who sold them their house of furniture. They will think that there was something special about him, because there was. I wonder if the children of the family will tell *their* children about this special man and his willingness to serve. Perhaps they will even retain an old rocking chair, pass it from generation to generation, and tell the story of the man whose store was a front for God.

Many people think the purpose of work is to make money, but I know people who have accepted lower paying jobs and who have turned down promotions in order to remain in positions that allow them the best opportunity to be about the Father's business. The tragedy around work is that we believe it is about making ends meet. The circle that enfolds work is much greater than getting. It is an opportunity to give. It is not just about making a living; it is also about letting God make something of our lives.

The Purpose of Work

Let us consider that our work is a place where our purpose and mission can live and where our gifts can be given. Kahlil Gibran, in his inspired work *The Prophet,* declared that "work is love made visible." Truly, this is the mission of every human being.

Every successful business has this quality. The word *love* may never be used, but it is present as an attitude of service. Customers are served by the employees, and the employees are valued and served by management.

No job makes us love, but our employment is a place where we can bring love to others. When we do this, we come alive. Remember, God is seeking expression. All aspects of human experience can be where God appears. This is also true of our employment. We spend many hours at our jobs. We can be present in order to receive our paycheck at the end of the month, or we can show up each day to perform our tasks. However, our work can be more than money and tasks; it can be a doorway through which Spirit does Its work.

This is the way it is with spiritual things. We think the job is about publishing books, for instance, when in Truth it is about personal relationships and sharing a message that can be helpful to others or that entertains them. It is easy to focus on the books and forget the value of relationships and the gift a good book can be to the reader.

Work's purpose is not to sustain earthly existence. It is not solely an avenue for health benefits, paid vacations, and salary. Let us not work so we can walk through the door of our homes relieved that another day has ended, but let us go to our

place of employment and give ourselves to our
tasks with the understanding that we can be a doorway through which Spirit may enter to do Its work.

Sacred Work

Sacred work is the act of bringing God into what
we do. God is always present, of course, but we
may not be aware of the Presence that is eager to
pour Itself into our lives and what we do. Whenever
we awaken to God's presence or remember that we
are not alone, we "bring" Spirit to the workplace.

It is quite possible to be away from work but still
be about our Father's business. A man and his co-
workers were rushing to the train station so they
could catch a commuter train and go home. While
passing through the station, the man and his com-
panions knocked over an applecart serviced by a
young boy. The men hesitated but then rushed on,
because if they had stopped they would have
missed their train.

All the men were seated on the train, and it was
about to pull out of the station. One man stood up
and announced that he had to go back and help the
boy pick up the apples. He left the train, and the
train left the station. Returning to the applecart,
the man could see the boy on his hands and knees
groping for the apples. He was blind. The busi-

nessman began to help the young boy. After they were finished, the boy asked him, "Are you Jesus?"

God's work is never done. There are no vacations, no fifteen-minute breaks, but our Creator is no taskmaster. Sacred work is joy, the joy which the man felt for a deed well done and the joy which the boy felt in believing that perhaps Jesus was helping him.

Can you see that when we think of work in this way, what counts is not what we do, but being present in a way which allows Spirit to act and do Its work? There is a sacredness to this activity. It fills our lives with meaning.

Silence Is the Door

Every job has its skills to be learned and tasks to be performed. As we skillfully complete our tasks, the work gets done. The question is, What skills must we learn and what tasks are we to perform that will allow Spirit's work to be accomplished? How does the "door" form, so that the Presence which is always with us may no longer be dormant, but a dominant force for good in our lives and the world?

Surprisingly, it is silence and stillness that invite Spirit to do Its work. I have a custom where I work that many people share with me. Whenever I have a

meeting in my office, I invite those who are present
to rest in stillness and silence for five minutes before
we begin our meeting. This simple act is an ac-
knowledgment of the one Presence and one Power.
The stillness is a letting go and is a practical expression of the thought that *I of myself can do nothing.*

Silence appears empty and of little use, but it is
a true friend and an ally in the workplace. Once, an
associate and I were going to be interviewed by a
person who had proven himself to be a hostile re-
porter. Our public relations director prepared both
of us for the meeting, but we invited the Spirit of
harmony and peace to make Itself known as the
three of us sat in silence twenty minutes prior to
the meeting.

The human tendency is to believe that something
must be done before God will act through us. Action
must be taken. This is not true, for action must be
received. First, there needs to be a turning to God
and a total receptivity by being silent and still. Then
there will be action that comes from the stillness.
Action is given and thankfully received, not taken.

Years ago a woman invited me to lunch near her
workplace. She told me she had something she
wanted to show me. After our meal, we entered the
bank where she worked as a manager. She took me
to a small room that had been set aside by the com-
pany, so the employees could "come . . . apart . . . a

while" anytime they thought they needed to be still and to center themselves for the tasks at hand. From this kind of management, comes creativity and compassion. Companies and institutions that enact policies like these will lead us into the next millennium. Not everyone is blessed to be working in an environment that endorses silence, but I believe any worker can bring this gift to the workplace. Anyone can pause for twenty seconds, a monastic moment, and acknowledge the presence of God within them. Anyone who has a ten-minute break can dedicate a portion of it to oneness with the One.

Can you see that the essence of work is not finding the perfect job? It is allowing Spirit an opportunity to do Its work wherever you are employed.Whenever this comes to be, sacred work is performed, for anything done from an awareness of the Presence is sacred. Appearances will declare that nothing has changed, but the person performing a task from an awareness of the Infinite and those who come in contact with this person will *know* that something is different. They may not be able to put their feelings into words, but they know God is at work.

From the Mountain to the Valley

Remember the story of Jesus in which he took James, John, and Peter to a high place and was

transfigured before them? The disciples wanted to
build altars to commemorate this event. Jesus
wanted to return to the valley, and when he did, he
allowed his Father to do a healing work.

This is the way it is when we live a life of meaning. We give ourselves to Spirit. We are still and
silent, and then we act. We leave the high place and
journey to the valley and become a blessing.

Entertaining the Christ

Let us not hold the life of the contemplative to be
more blessed than that of the activist. Also, let us
not consider the life of action to be more practical
than the life of one who is committed to silence and
stillness. This is the lesson of the story of Mary,
Martha, and Jesus.

Mary and Martha were sisters. Apparently, Jesus
often visited their home. Hospitality in Eastern culture is vitally important, and during Jesus' visits,
Martha would insure that everyone was cared for
and that all their needs were met. Mary would sit
at Jesus' feet and listen to him. In the episode
recorded in Luke 10:38–42, Martha complains to
Jesus that Mary is not helping. Jesus replies:
"Martha, Martha, you are anxious and troubled
about many things; one thing is needful. Mary has
chosen the good portion" (Lk 10:41–42).

It appears as though Jesus is endorsing Mary's behavior, but there is more to this story. Mystical insight states that both Mary and Martha are necessary to entertain the Christ. Both contemplation and activity are vital if humanity is to honor its true identity and be about the Father's business.

Martha's problem was not that she was working too hard, but that she condemned her sister. I believe that if Mary would have said to Jesus, "Tell my sister to cease her work and listen to your message of Truth," the Master would have also said to her, "Mary, Mary, you are anxious and troubled about many things."

If Martha's work had been a product of contemplation and silence, that is, if her actions would have risen out of an awareness of the Presence, she would not have been anxious and troubled. Martha's work wed to stillness would have been the best of both worlds. This kind of work is an act of worship. Our desk, our lathe, our cab is an altar where people are blessed and treated as though they were the Christ.

Begin the Divine Work Today

It is our destiny to be about our Father's business. Our work can be sacred if we will begin in stillness and silence. Start where you are. You do not need a high-powered job. Do simple things for God's glory. Don't ask for more to do; do what you do with joy, and more will be given. Listen before you act.

Brother Lawrence, a seventeenth-century Carmelite monk, is a supreme example of someone who found the sacred in the simple things. His work was in the kitchen. In fact, for his whole career he worked in the monastery kitchen. At first, he resented his work, but then he decided to do everything he did for God's glory. He began to wed his work to the contemplation of Spirit. After a time, his oneness with God filled him with such ecstasy that he reported he was feeling "joys so continual and so great that I can scarce contain them!"

Religious leaders began to come to him for advice. They sensed the presence of God at work in him. Imagine the meals he must have served—simple, yet sacred—just like the service you are destined to render.

Mile Markers

- Work is an opportunity to give.
- Work is the act of letting God make something of our lives.
- Sacred work is the act of bringing God into what you do.
- Sacred work is action born of stillness.
- Do simple things for God's glory.

Adventure Five

Sacred Work

The beginning is the most important part of the work.

—Plato

Who is it that performs sacred work? Is it only the priests, rabbis, and ministers of the world? Where is sacred work performed? Only in the cathedrals, temples, mosques and churches of the world? I am a minister, but I want nothing to do with this kind of sacred work, for it is too confining and exclusive.

Instead, I want sacred work to move from the religious community into the tiny hamlets of Vietnam and the skyscrapers of New York. I yearn for the day when the fisherman casting his nets and the farmer sowing his seeds will experience a reverence exceeding what is felt when he kneels before the altar to worship.

There is a tendency to believe that sacred work is religious. It is the work itself that is sacred. This is not true. It is the beginning that determines if work is sacred or not. A religious service may be sacred or it may not. Its sacredness depends upon the consciousness out of which the service is given, not what is said or done. Motivation is the key. *The beginning is the most important part of the work.* I remember receiving a Christmas card from a person I had never met. It came from the man who collected the trash at our home every Wednesday. I had never seen him, but his simple "Season's Greetings" told me he saw his work differently from most people. I sensed that the beginning of his work was in the unseen realm. I don't know if it is true or not, but I choose to believe his day begins with God, and from this beginning comes sacred work.

Soul-Talk

 I begin my work in silence.
Write this three times and repeat each day during this Adventure.

1. _____

2. _____

3. _____

Soul-Thoughts

After contemplation, write down your thoughts.

1. What is the Father's work?

2. Is your work a storefront for God? If not, how could it be?

Seeds are true to their nature. No matter where they are sown, they attempt to grow. In the high, arid, and rocky places of the world, there is vegetation. The short growing season stunts the growth of these trees and plants, but they still bloom where they are planted. Our place of work may not seem ideal, but the real question is not what the work will do for us, but what we can bring to the job. *Will we be true to our nature and bloom where we are planted, or will we make excuses why we are not more than we appear to be?*

3. *What can you do to make your workplace an avenue of Spirit's expression?*

4. *Are you willing to believe that your work is not as important as the consciousness out of which it is performed?*

5. *Are you so busy that you don't have time to be still?*

6. *If there were only one reason why a person would be anxious and troubled on the job, what would it be?*

Off the Main Trail

If your employer asked you to come up with five recommendations to make your work sacred, what would you recommend?

Stepping-Stone

 Mary and Martha entertained Jesus. If you had been present as one of these women, *which one would you have been? What would you have said, and what would Jesus have said to you?*

I begin my work in silence.

Chapter Six

There's Work for You to Do

Can you sense it? There's work for you to do. You can make a contribution to the world, and your needs can be supplied, without making them the object of your existence. This was the experience of Charles and Myrtle Fillmore, co-founders of the Unity movement. They worked tirelessly in service to God and humanity, and their needs were abundantly met. A covenant was prelude to this way of life. It was signed by Charles and Myrtle on December 7, 1892, but was not made public until after their deaths.

Dedication and Covenant

We, Charles Fillmore and Myrtle Fillmore, husband and wife, hereby dedicate ourselves, our time, our money, all we have and all we expect to have, to the Spirit of Truth, and through it, to the Society of Silent Unity.

It being understood and agreed that the said Spirit of Truth shall render unto us an equivalent for this dedication, in peace of mind, health of body, wisdom,

*understanding, love, life and an abundant supply of
all things necessary to meet every want without our
making any of these things the object of our existence.
In the presence of the Conscious Mind of Christ
Jesus, this 7th day of December, A.D. 1892.*

Obviously, the Fillmores' work was spiritual in
nature. This was their call to service. Their talents
and gifts led them to the work of prayer and spiritual education. Most of us don't have their talents.
However, the Presence seeks expression, and this
expression is not limited to religious endeavors. A
consciousness of God is a force for good, just as
much in a hospital, real estate office, or classroom
as it is in a church. Regardless of the work, the
worker can be attuned to Spirit.

In Search of Work

Some of us are unemployed, but we are not out
of work. Our purpose is the same whether we are
employed or not; it is to know God. We still have a
mission to fulfill whether we report to a place of
employment or an employment office, in hope of
being placed in a job. Our mission does not come
into being when we have a job and disappear when
our job is no more. Our mission is to allow Spirit to
express Itself in, through, and *as* us. Purpose and
mission continue always as a part of the eternal

spiritual journey. And when anyone is attuned to Spirit and therefore true to his or her purpose and mission, Spirit will put this individual to work.

Through the years, I have counseled many people in search of employment. I have told them that their search was for something greater. It was for God. Their unemployment was a call and an opportunity to return to their spiritual roots and to re-establish their purpose of knowing their Creator and their mission of allowing God's expression.

I suggested that they open themselves to experience the Presence as their Source—their Source, because out of this experience would come security and well-being. A consciousness of God as Source also usually manifests itself as an avenue of prosperity—a job. In addition, I suggested that they be willing to experience the Presence as wisdom. Experience had taught me that sometimes people obtained employment in which there was no challenge or creativity. They had a job, but little else.

When a person comes to know God as wisdom, creativity abounds. You see, a job seeker does not want just a job; the person also wants to make a contribution to the world. The seeker wants to know that his or her work counts; it matters.

A consciousness of wisdom would also prove helpful, because in nearly every example I am aware of, the person would receive not one job offer, but several. Obviously, wisdom and guidance are necessary to determine where the individual should serve.

No one can force an experience of the Presence. Intent and motivation are our first contributions to the process. We lift our attention from our need for employment and let it rest in our desire to know God. This is a call for our old friends—stillness and silence. Receptivity and persistence are now our work. The gift of God that comes as an experience of the Presence is out of our hands, but *at* hand. This is Spirit's work, and it comes through grace.

Eventually, a sense of security comes. Peace prevails. Now it is time for us to be sensitive to opportunities and to guidance that come from within or from the world. A person may call us and tell us about a job opportunity. An idea that calls us to action may fill our minds. A first step is often taken that thrusts us into the unknown. Our faithful first step reveals our next step and our next.

I'll bet you didn't know the unemployed had so much work to do. And there is more. The person in search of meaning must be willing to discover and initially give away his gift. This is the nature of any gift; it is given away, and yet it remains. I have seen musicians and artists provide their services free of charge, and I have seen new careers blossom out of this spirit of giving. Initially, they did not need just a job; they also needed to place a new value on their talents.

However, all of this spiritual work does not mean that the person in search of employment does not provide prospective employers a resume or that he does not attend job interviews. The ways of the world are honored, but so are the ways of Spirit.

Even the employed often search for work, for some of us are in jobs we do not like. There is no fulfillment—of course not, for no job *can* fulfill us. Fulfillment is not the role of employment. Instead, a job is a place to find that we are filled with God. It is a place where we can give the gift of our talents and realize what we give away remains with us. In Truth, giving of ourselves even strengthens our gift. Our purpose deepens. Our mission becomes more clear, and our talents expand and become more appreciated by those we serve.

The "Work" of the Retired

When we are young, we wonder why we are here. What is our purpose? Is there something special for us to do? The challenges of life often cause us to forget these important questions. As we draw closer to death, we begin to ask the questions once more.

The questions are rephrased, but they are essentially the same. What was it all about? Did my life have meaning? Did I make a contribution? What am I to do with my remaining days?

When a person looks at the past, these questions can be answered, but the past is not all there is. A future lies ahead, and it can be different from what has gone before. It can be a crowning jewel of a life well lived.

These mature individuals have worked, usually for many years. They don't want a job, but they do want to live a life of meaning. These dear friends sense that they have gifts to give. Perhaps there are even new gifts to uncover and give to the world.

In Hinduism, there is a stage of life that a person may pursue after the first grandchild is born. At this time, both men and women may leave home and give their lives fully to the spiritual search. They deepen their consciousness of God and life. Detachment is learned, but they do not remain detached from the world. Eventually, they return from their quest more at peace and more attuned to the Presence.

Our culture does not endorse this approach to living, but in principle this practice can be lived by anyone who is retired. Spiritual consciousness becomes primary, and through this increased awareness, the person becomes an example of how to live. They show us how to face challenges and how to treat others. No one needs to tell a mature individual how to do these things. In their heart of hearts, they know. It simply must be done.

If there is a desire to make God the center of one's life, let there first be stillness and silence—just as there is in the business world. The source of life remains the same and the doorway through which the Presence enters is as it has always been—stillness and silence.

This requires a shift in identity. This is where many retired people struggle, for their identity is often rooted in the past and what *was* done. Now they no longer work, and therefore they feel lost. They don't know who they are. The mother no longer mothers, or she may attempt to—with negative results. The attention may shift to the grandchildren, and there is joy, but it should not supplant the spiritual search. If there is ever a time in a person's life to experience purpose and mission, this is the time!

Life is without meaning for those who do not shift their identity from what *was* done to that which endures and is eternal. I recall learning that high-ranking military officers with immense responsibilities often die within a decade of their retirement. These are young people with much of their lives before them, but the responsibilities of maintaining the garden do not compare to the command of an aircraft carrier.

Retirement is often a time for travel and fun for those who can afford it, but this does not make life more meaningful. The kingdom of God waits to be explored, and in the journey, there is true joy. It is enlivening to see the wonders of the world, but we come alive when we witness the wonders of Spirit at work in our lives and the lives of others.

God Has Work for You to Do

Time and circumstance do not place us beyond a life of meaning. Our many years educate us in the ways of the world, but their most potent message is that we are spiritual beings living in a spiritual universe. Earthly circumstances change. Many of the experiences challenge us. They cause us to seek solutions, and if we are good at problem solving, life seems to progress and expand. However, let us not allow circumstances to push aside the subtle proddings of Spirit. We are more than flesh and blood and more than what we do. We are potentially stargates through which the Divine may enter and express Itself.

We are made for more than earthly work, but if we are to find our reason for being, we must turn

from what we have known for so long. God is calling us: *"Listen. . . . Be still and know. . . . There is
work for you to do."* Earthly voices will not call it
"grand" but what could be more grand than a life
lived from a consciousness of the One!

Mile Markers

- When we are attuned to God, God will put us to work.
- No job can fulfill us.
- A life of meaning comes to those whose identity rests in the eternal.

Adventure Six

There's Work for You to Do

Shun those studies in which the work that results dies with the worker.

—Leonardo da Vinci

For most of our lives we work—five, six, or seven days a week and many hours a day: nine to five, eight to five, even seven to seven. Then the day comes when there is no need to rise early in the morning, for we are unemployed. We have retired or are currently out of work. Habit causes us to awaken at the same early hour, but now there is nothing to do. Or is there?

Life can become more clear and balanced when this morning comes. Now is the time to remember we are *human beings*. Prior to this early morning hour, each of us had been a *human doing* his job.

The past and our thoughts about it matter little now. This is a new day, for it is an opportunity— not an opportunity to step into the world, but an opportunity to be filled with divine energies and purpose as we step into God's kingdom. Balance is the potential blessing of this day and the days to follow.

Work was once something we did. Ideally, we sought to be a blessing to the world. Now we become explorers of an interior realm. And when we return from our journey, we will have much to share with those with eyes to see and ears to hear. This is what happened to Jesus. His life was an adventure into a land foreign to most of humanity. He returned to tell strange tales and truths about it and about us.

The trailhead has been marked. Let us begin. There is little we need to take with us—a desire to know God, a yearning to love, a willingness to allow Spirit to express Itself, an enthusiasm for service, and humility. We will discover other provisions along the way. Such is the work of the one who rises on a new day with nothing to do!

Soul-Talk

God has work for me to do.
Write this three times and repeat each day during this Adventure.

1. _____

2. _____

3. _____

Soul-Thoughts

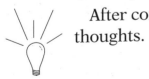 After contemplation, write down your thoughts.

1. *What are the purpose, mission, and "work" of the unemployed?*

2. *What spiritual approach would you recommend to someone who is looking for a job?*

3. *What are the characteristics of an individual whose worth and identity are in his employment?*

4. *What is the role of silence and stillness in work?*

5. *What is the "work" of the retired?*

6. Assume that you want to begin that "work," either upon retirement or through a special opportunity as in the Hindu tradition. *What is your first step? Your second step?*

Off the Main Trail

Write a covenant that expresses your willingness to work in partnership with God.

Stepping-Stone

 Share one of your gifts without remuneration. *What happened? How does it feel?*

God has work for me to do.

Future Quest

If You Had Never Lived

The Tree of Life

We are a species of purpose. Our creation was
not by chance. We may have evolved from cosmic
dust, but every pathway leading to our conception
and subsequent growth in consciousness was conceived by God. Infinite wisdom always has a reason, but we may not see it, because our attention is
upon the world and its promises. Therefore, we fail
to perceive God's promise of creativity, compassion,
peace, and power.

Imagine the life lived by one of us who has
danced with the question *Why?* and felt life's
rhythms and harmony as purpose. A few of these
lives have been lived, but we are *all* called to this
life. Whenever one of us awakens to our purpose of
knowing God, our world expands and we know not
only our Creator, but also our mission. Previously
hidden gifts and talents emerge, and we go to work.
There are days when we would rather remain at
home, but for the most part, work is a joy. We feel
God's pleasure and make no claim that we are the

doer. We know that we of ourselves can do nothing. It is the Spirit of the universe that is at work.

Now imagine the creativity, compassion, peace, and power of the many. Something wonderful would come into the world. Jesus gave us this promise: "For where two or three are gathered in my name, there am I in the midst of them" (Mt. 18:20). When humanity gathers its forces in a united purpose and mission, something even greater than the sum total of our united energies emerges from within us. This unity of purpose causes our tree of life to sprout new growth. The evolution of the race marches in a new direction. Even in the winter, this tree will be heavy laden with the fruits of Spirit.

A new species is evolving. Our outer appearance may be as it is today, but in the reality that is consciousness, we will be different—compelled by divine energies which show themselves as a mission to assist one another, concerned not only for ourselves, but for the many. Our preference will be that all gifts and talents be shared. This new creation will bring Spirit into all areas of human endeavor. All labor will be sacred, because it is not *we* who work—it is Spirit. It will be a better world, because we had the courage to dance with the question *Why?* This is our destiny, and it unfolds one person at a time.

Divine Friendship

Sometimes it is the allure of the world that causes us to forsake our true purpose and try to develop our own mission and work. Gifts and talents are often misused, and when we work, we feel no pleasure. At other times, the challenges and trauma of life cause us to forget that we are spiritual beings created for a spiritual purpose. We are orphaned by life's difficulties. We wonder if there is a purpose for our being. This is the winter of our life, but spring is near.

The fact that we wonder why we are here is the first sign of the coming of a new season. If life is treating us harshly and seems without rhyme or reason, it is because we do not know our purpose. We do not yet know that within every crisis is a call to purpose. We are being asked to remember who we are and why we are here.

Most of us spend our time trying to alleviate our anxiety and anguish. This is understandable, but ridding ourselves of pain is not our purpose. Our challenge is not the issue, nor is our work to find a way to overcome it. The challenge is a call to return to center, where the Presence waits in silent repose.

Still we may persist in our way. Some of us become angry with God. Why won't this mighty Spirit act on our behalf? Because God is not our servant;

God is our beloved, and *we* are beloved of God. A divine friendship awaits us. The fruit of knowing God is discovering ourselves and what Spirit can do in, through, and *as* us.

Falling in Love

Human beings speak of falling in love, but our joy is *resting* in love. Remember how it was when you first were in love with someone. You wanted to spend all your time together. You wanted to know everything about each other. A divine friendship requires that we give daily attention to the Presence. A consciousness of the One becomes a part of us. Then, when the traumas of life come, we have a pool or reservoir of spiritual awareness and understanding out of which we can act and live. When there is no consciousness of the One, it is like trying to make a withdrawal from a checking account in which we have made no deposits. However, the good news is that we can begin anew.

Our salvation is that our spiritual identity is untouched by our anxiety and difficulties. Things we have done and left undone, said and not said, do not touch our spiritual nature. Acts perpetrated upon us impact our surface selves, but the pattern of perfection remains. Our new beginning is to turn Godward and ask, *Why am I here?*

Spirit interprets this question not as a request to

know why we are in a particular situation, but why we are here upon the earth. Why *are* we? This question is answered. Just as it was for me long ago when the cursor on my computer locked up and would not move, so it is for every human being. I looked to God and the answer came—*"Know Me."*

If You Had Never Lived

In Frank Capra's movie classic *It's a Wonderful Life*, the impact of a person's life upon the lives of others is explored. As the movie nears its conclusion, George Bailey, played by James Stewart, contemplates his suicide. An angel allows him to see what would happen if he had never lived. This exploration brings our hero to his senses, and he is surprised to learn that he is valued and loved by the townspeople.

No one can tell what the world would be like if we had never lived or if our life had ended prematurely. The specifics cannot be known; but one thing is sure—we can make a difference.

A person who seeks to know God, an individual who knows the reason for being, is a stargate through which the divine light comes into the world. Two things are sure. If you had never lived or had never experienced your purpose, the world would be less for it. However, because you live and dance with the question *Why?* the world is a better place.

About the Author

Jim Rosemergy serves as executive vice president of Unity School of Christianity at its world headquarters in Unity Village, Missouri. Jim also serves on the Unity Movement Advisory Council, a joint committee of the Association of Unity Churches and Unity School of Christianity.

Jim was born on July 13, 1947, in Elizabeth City, North Carolina. Because his father was in the military, he moved frequently, going to twelve different schools in twelve years. He lived in numerous places along the Gulf and East coasts, from Mobile, Alabama, to Cape Cod, Massachusetts. An athletic boy and natural leader, he found himself excelling at tennis, captaining his tennis team at Old Dominion College (now Old Dominion University), where he also earned a B.S. in chemistry. Jim saw combat in North Vietnam as a naval aviator and flew more than one hundred missions.

Reverend Rosemergy was ordained a Unity minister in 1976. He pioneered a ministry in Raleigh, North Carolina, that grew from eighteen people to over three hundred in seven years, with an emphasis on prayer (an activity which continues to be at the heart of his ministry). Next, Jim served Unity Church of Truth in Spokane, Washington, where his emphasis was on spiritual awakening and assisting people in their quests for purpose and meaning in life.

Prior to returning to Unity Village, Jim served as senior minister at the co-founders' church, Unity Temple on the Plaza in Kansas City, Missouri. In 1987–88, he was elected president of the Association of Unity Churches.

Jim is also a writer of numerous articles and poems, as well as nine books and nine cassette albums. His column "The Spiritual Journey" appears monthly in *Unity Magazine*. His books include the best-selling *A Daily Guide to Spiritual Living*, as well as the more recent *The Sacred Human* and *A Closer Walk With God*.

Jim and Nancy, his wife of over twenty-eight years, have two grown sons, Jamie and Ben.

Printed in the U.S.A.

11-1769-10M-10-98